W9-BMD-748

MERCURY

by Ariel Kazunas

CHERRY LAKE PUBLISHING * ANN ARBOR, MICHIGAN

Published in the United States of America by Cherry Lake Publishing
Ann Arbor, Michigan
www.cherrylakepublishing.com

Content Adviser: Dr. Tobias Owen, University of Hawaii Institute for Astronomy

Photo Credits: Cover and page 4, ©Orlando Florin Rosu/Dreamstime.com; cover and page 6, ©Sergey Vasilyev/Shutterstock, Inc.; cover and page 12, ©Plutonius 3d/Shutterstock, Inc.; cover and page 16, ©Igor Kovalchuk/Shutterstock, Inc.; page 8, ©Matamu/Shutterstock, Inc.; pages 10, 14, and 18, ©NASA; page 20, ©Luis Stortini Sabor aka CVADRAT/Shutterstock, Inc.

LIBRARY OF CONGRESS CATALOGING-IN-PUBLICATION DATA
Kazunas, Ariel.
 Mercury/by Ariel Kazunas.
     p. cm.—(21st century junior library)
 Includes bibliographical references and index.
 ISBN-13: 978-1-61080-088-4 (lib. bdg.)
 ISBN-10: 1-61080-088-5 (lib. bdg.)
 1. Mercury (Planet)—Juvenile literature. I. Title. II. Series.
 QB611.K39 2011
 523.41—dc22   2010052378

Cherry Lake Publishing would like to acknowledge the work of
The Partnership for 21st Century Skills.
Please visit www.21stcenturyskills.org *for more information.*

Printed in the United States of America
Corporate Graphics Inc.
July 2011
CLFA09

CONTENTS

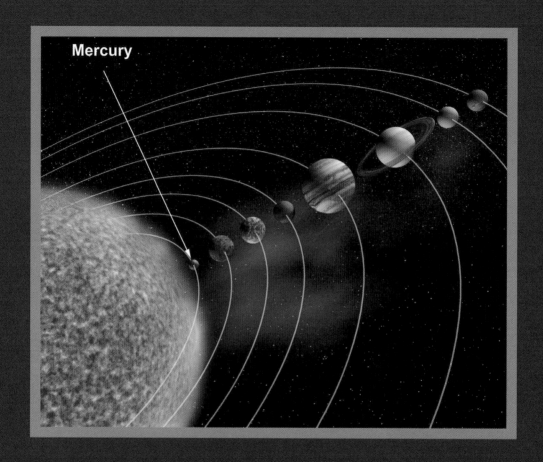

Mercury

Mercury is tiny compared to any other planet in
our solar system.

Neighbors with the Sun

Our **solar system** is made up of eight planets. They travel around the Sun. The planet closest to the Sun is called Mercury.

Mercury is the smallest planet in our solar system. It is about the same size as Earth's Moon.

The Roman god Mercury is often shown with wings on his hat or shoes.

Humans discovered Mercury at least 5,000 years ago. They named the planet after a **Roman god**. Mercury was a messenger god. He was known for moving very fast. The planet got its name because it moves very fast, too.

Look!

You can see Mercury in the sky on some nights. You don't even need a telescope. But you do need to know where to look. A librarian can help you find out where you can spot this tiny planet.

Mercury travels a shorter distance around the Sun than any other planet does.

Years and Days

Mercury **orbits** the Sun faster than any other planet does. This is because it is so close to the Sun. It gets as close as 36 million miles (58 million kilometers) from the Sun. That's more than 57 million miles (92 million km) closer than Earth gets to the Sun.

Earth takes longer to circle the sun
than Mercury does.

The time it takes for a planet to orbit the Sun one time is called a year. Mercury's small orbit makes its years very short. A year on Earth is 365 days long. A year on Mercury is only 88 Earth days long.

Mercury rotates counterclockwise on its axis.

The time it takes a planet to **rotate** on its **axis** one full time is called a day. Mercury rotates very slowly. The only planet in our solar system that rotates slower is Venus. This means Mercury's days are very long. One day on Mercury is as long as 59 Earth days!

Ask Questions!

How many days make up one year on Mercury? You can use math to find the answer. Ask a teacher or parent to help if you aren't sure how to start.

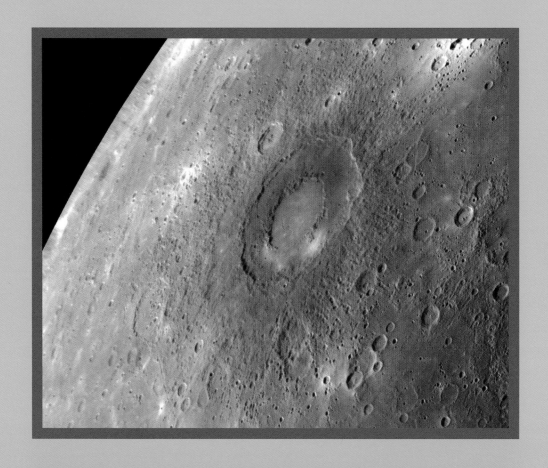

Craters cover most of Mercury's surface.

All About the Atmosphere

Mercury's **atmosphere** is very thin. Objects from space can pass right through it. Big objects make **craters** on Mercury's surface when they crash. Mercury is covered with craters of all sizes.

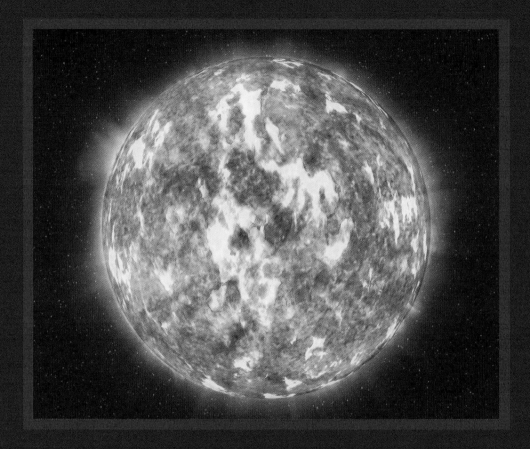

The Sun's heat makes Mercury a very warm place during the day.

Mercury can reach 800 degrees Fahrenheit (427 degrees Celsius) during the day. Mercury gets this hot because it is so close to the Sun.

Temperatures can drop to –300°F (–184°C) at night. No other planet has such a wide range of temperatures.

Make a Guess!

Why does it get so cold at night on Mercury? Remember that Mercury's days are very long. This means its nights are very long, too!

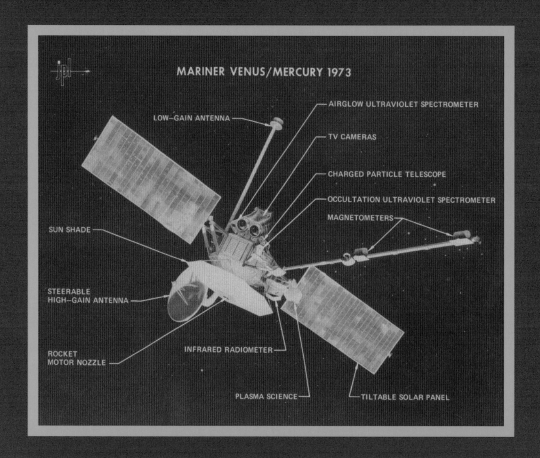

MARINER VENUS/MERCURY 1973

LOW-GAIN ANTENNA

AIRGLOW ULTRAVIOLET SPECTROMETER

TV CAMERAS

CHARGED PARTICLE TELESCOPE

OCCULTATION ULTRAVIOLET SPECTROMETER

MAGNETOMETERS

SUN SHADE

STEERABLE
HIGH-GAIN ANTENNA

ROCKET
MOTOR NOZZLE

INFRARED RADIOMETER

PLASMA SCIENCE

TILTABLE SOLAR PANEL

The many parts of *Mariner 10* helped to collect a
lot of different information.

Looking for Clues

Scientists sent a spacecraft called *Mariner 10* to Mercury in 1973. It sent back lots of information about Mercury.

Scientists sent another spacecraft called *Messenger* in 2004. *Messenger* has helped them learn even more about Mercury.

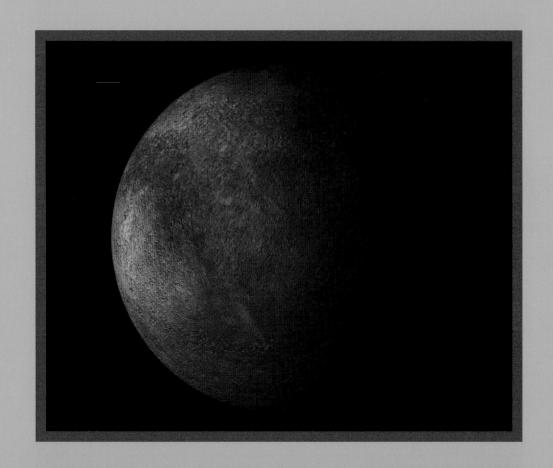

Mercury still holds many secrets.

There is still a lot that scientists don't know about Mercury. Even *Mariner 10* and *Messenger* have not seen some parts of its surface.

Scientists will continue trying to learn all they can about Mercury. What will they find out next?

Create!

Do you think the rest of Mercury looks like the parts we have already seen? Try drawing a picture of Mercury. Don't forget to include a lot of craters!

GLOSSARY

atmosphere (AT-muhss-fihr) the gases or air surrounding a planet

axis (AK-siss) an imaginary line that goes through an object and around which the object turns

craters (KRAY-turz) holes caused by one object in space hitting another

orbits (OR-bits) travels in a path around a central point

Roman god (ROH-muhn GOD) one of many beings thought to have power over people and nature; the Romans were people who lived long ago in Rome or places ruled by Rome

rotate (ROH-tayt) spin

scientists (SYE-uhn-tists) people who study nature and make discoveries

solar system (SOH-lur SISS-tuhm) a star, such as the Sun, and all the planets and moons that move around it

FIND OUT MORE

BOOKS

Aguilar, David A. *11 Planets: A New View of the Solar System.* Washington, DC: National Geographic Society, 2008.

Landau, Elaine. *Mercury.* New York: Children's Press, 2007.

Vogt, Gregory. *Mercury.* Minneapolis: Lerner Publications, 2010.

WEB SITES

HubbleSite Gallery

hubblesite.org/gallery
Take a look at some cool pictures of outer space.

NASA: Solar System Exploration

solarsystem.nasa.gov/kids
Check out these fun activities from NASA.

Space.com—Our Solar System: Facts, Formation and Discovery

www.space.com/solarsystem/
Learn more about the objects in our solar system and how they were formed.

INDEX

ABOUT THE AUTHOR

Ariel Kazunas lives on the Oregon coast, writing books for kids and working at the Sitka Center for Art and Ecology. She has also worked for several nonprofit magazines. Ariel loves exploring our planet, Earth—especially by hand, foot, bike, and boat—and camping out under the stars.